AUDIO
ACCESS
INCLUDED

VIOLA

THE LION KING

T0081434

Audio arrangements by Peter Deneff

To access audio visit:
www.halleonard.com/mylibrary

Enter Code
2298-5258-7740-2629

Motion Picture Artwork TM & Copyright © 2019 Disney

ISBN 978-1-5400-6575-9

Visit Hal Leonard Online at
www.halleonard.com

Contact us:
Hal Leonard
7777 West Bluemound Road
Milwaukee, WI 53213
Email: info@halleonard.com

In Europe, contact:
Hal Leonard Europe Limited
42 Wigmore Street
Marylebone, London, W1U 2RN
Email: info@halleonardeurope.com

In Australia, contact:
Hal Leonard Australia Pty. Ltd.
4 Lentara Court
Cheltenham, Victoria, 3192 Australia
Email: info@halleonard.com.au

CONTENTS

CAN YOU FEEL THE LOVE TONIGHT

VIOLA

Music by ELTON JOHN
Lyrics by TIM RICE

CIRCLE OF LIFE

VIOLA

Music by ELTON JOHN
Lyrics by TIM RICE

HAKUNA MATATA

VIOLA

Music by ELTON JOHN
Lyrics by TIM RICE

I JUST CAN'T WAIT TO BE KING

VIOLA

Music by ELTON JOHN
Lyrics by TIM RICE

HE LIVES IN YOU

VIOLA

Music and Lyrics by MARK MANCINA,
JAY RIFKIN and LEBOHANG MORAKE

THE LION SLEEPS TONIGHT

Viola

New Lyrics and Revised Music by GEORGE DAVID WEISS,
HUGO PERETTI and LUIGI CREATORE

NEVER TOO LATE

VIOLA

Music by ELTON JOHN
Lyrics by TIM RICE

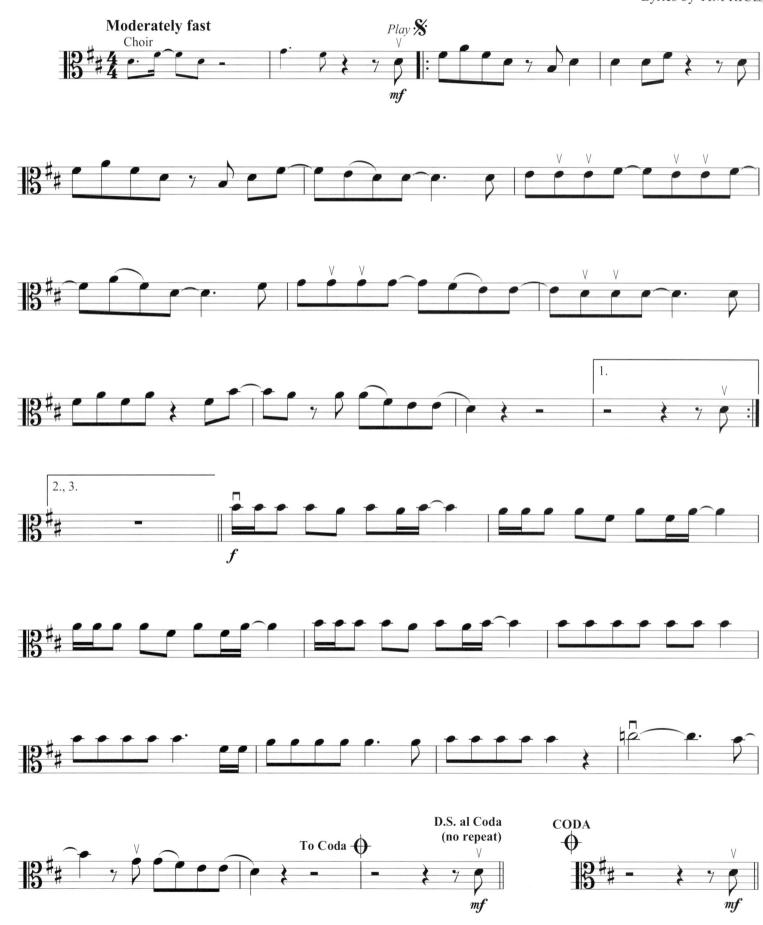

STAMPEDE

VIOLA

Composed by HANS ZIMMER

SPIRIT

VIOLA

Written by TIMOTHY McKENZIE
ILYA SALMANZADEH and BEYONCÉ

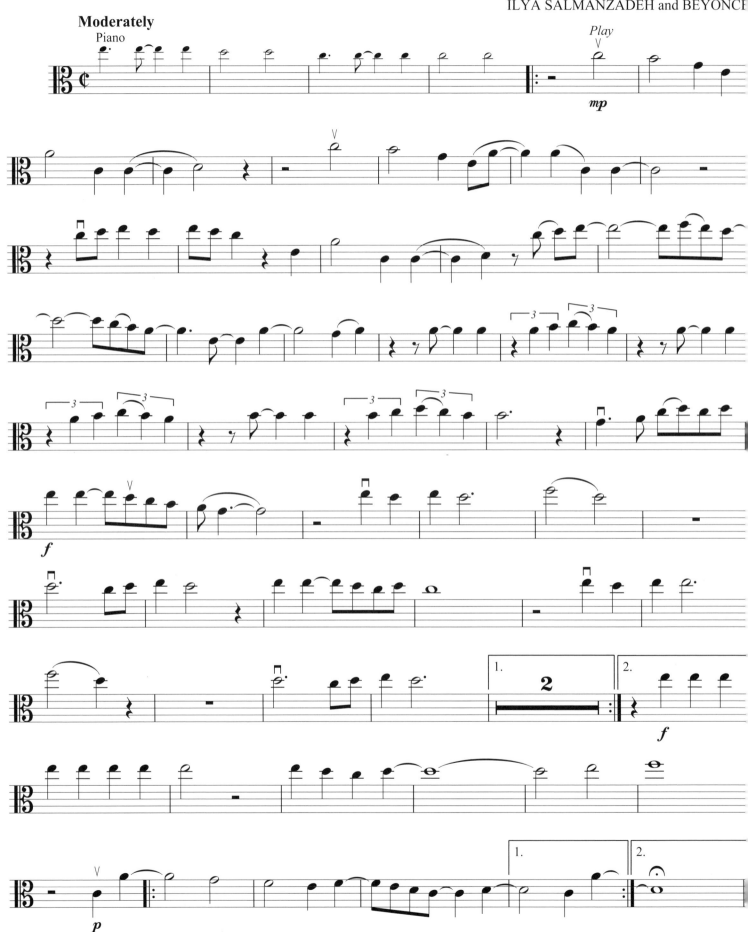